BOOK OF POEMS

You Are

EDEM Y. AGBLEY

Book of Poems
Vol. 1

YOU ARE

Edem Y. Agbley

Book of Poems: You Are
Vol. 1
Edem Y. Agbley

Copyright © 2014 by Edem Y. Agbley

All Rights Reserved. This book was self-published by the author Edem Y. Agbley through LIVE SMART SOLUTIONS LLC a Delaware company. No part of this book may be used or reproduced in any manner or format whatsoever without express written permission from the publisher except in the case of brief quotations embodied in critical articles or reviews.

This ebook is licensed for your personal enjoyment only. This ebook may not be resold or given away to others. If you would like to share this book with another person, please purchase an additional copy for each recipient.

If you're reading this book and didn't purchase it, or it was not purchased for your use only, then please return to your favorite ebook retailer and purchase your own copy. Thank you for respecting the hard work and efforts of the author.
Send feedback to: reviews@love4poems.com

Disclaimer and/or Legal Notices:
This book may contain sexually explicit material or topics that some readers would consider controversial or inappropriate for persons under the age of eighteen (18). The author, therefore, advises parental discretion when purchasing, reviewing, discussing or reading this material.
ISBN- 978-0692335758
Printed by CreateSpace, a DBA of On-Demand Publishing, LLC

Dedications:

To my lovely, talented, and awesome daughter Nailah. May your entire life be filled with nothing less than abundance.

To any and all individuals consciously making a positive impact in their community and the world.

Table of Contents

Introduction..vii

This Is A Dream..9

Smile Power..10

Hunger..11

Mr. Potato Head..12

It Ain't A Dollar Without A Penny..............13

Her..14

Crossroads..15

The 'hood..16

Final Thoughts 18

Acknowledgments......................................20

About the Author..22

About the Company....................................24

Introduction

Dear Readers,

It is my pleasure to bring you these selected poems which I've written over the course of this year, with one selected poem from my earlier poetic beginnings marked archives 2003. These poems are from the heart and were drawn from a higher place within me. Many influences assisted in shaping the words I'm sharing with you inside this book as I continue ahead on an ontological and transformational journey. My goal is not for you to simply read various characters and letters on a page, but to feel them intensely and become one with the dialogue. Hopefully this book will connect with you spiritually wherever you are, from my point of infinite awareness and answer a question you may have or more importantly, raise more powerful questions for you to discover.

This Is A Dream

Lucid thoughts and visions sway here and there like waves in the ocean, what you see is what you get. Find your essence amidst all the sounds and colors and let go.
This Is A Dream.

Nightmares of failure, demons and darkness intertwined with beings of light live timeless in your spirit. All equal love.
This Is A Dream.

Recurring situations you think you can't explain, kill your mind for a moment and see what's really happening inside your heart.
This Is A Dream.

You are all there is and ever will be, the good, bad, and the ugly. Self-discovery happens every nano second.
This Is A Dream.

Where can your dreams take you? You are the composer and the symphony.
This Is A Dream.

BE!

Smile Power

What can you do with a smile?

The power of a smile is mightier than your toughest foe.

It's the icing on the cake and the key that unlocks the door to
happiness on a sad day.

Smiling is contagious and adds delight to the eyes its bestowed upon.

If smiling represented wealth, would you be rich or poor?

Ask yourself, what can YOU do with a smile?

HUNGER

Against all odds, my will pushes through the blizzards, hurricanes, droughts and earthquakes. No matter what I'm faced with, my hunger will not allow my rest!

I must feed my mind, fill my body, and nourish my soul. Shall I lay in despair as my hunger pains grow stronger? Fuck you failure, under no circumstances will you defeat me!

You seek to kill my drive and destroy my future accomplishments NOW.
I laugh at your foolish attempts to deceive me into being a loser.

As in boxing, you may land a blow and even a stinging punch to my "gut" yet, before the sound of the bell, I've delivered the knockout for another victory! I'm starving with an unstoppable hunger for success!

Mr. Potato head

Have or have not? Don't be a have not struggling against another have not to have what a have has! Have as the have does. If you could replace what you had with what you have, would you have more? The have nots scrap for crumbs, while the haves feast at lavish buffets. Though you may think I'm speaking of food or a certain lifestyle, what I'm speaking of is a mindset!

IT AIN'T A DOLLAR WITHOUT A PENNY

The world is full of pieces that make a whole. Every insect, every species of animal, and the many different types of plants make up an awe inspiring world. In comes a tendency to label one thing less inferior to another; a hierarchy.

It ain't a dollar without a penny.

Shiny quarters dimes and nickels gleaming with opportunity, and the unwanted misused and neglected copper contraption. An outcast with the face pointed the opposite direction of all the other stars.

Walk down your local sidewalk and see him spewed all along the gutters and left for dead in between the cracks. Lifeless, most people step on it and keep walking saying, "it's only a penny"! How many times have you taken things in life for granted? Deemed one thing worthless compared to another? You cannot have a complete world without all its parts. Nothing is worthless in the universe.

It ain't a dollar without a penny.

HER

What is her name? All the words get lost inside the connected energy. The sun and moon combined with dazzling stars.

Smooth skin, deep eyes and toned thighs. I'm guided by my soul's vibrations to her volcanic sweet spot. Pure bliss as time ceases and heart rate increases.

Fingers twist and pull hair as two tongues tangle lead by the mind of desire and lust.
Her earth feels like the deepest waters and her sensual sandpit sinks and locks me into her grip. I shall die in her arms as sweat builds and we strain to savor this moment.

No longer can I nor her restrain from reaching the end of the line.
A race where no one wants to finish first. I pull she tugs as we get closer and closer to heaven yet the heat of hell is where we attempt to remain.

Recreation turns to procreation as we exchange a gush of goodness. I am her and she is me for an instant in time.
I Love Her.

Archives/2004

Crossroads

Life comes to a crossroad. Questions with no clear answer. Which way do you turn? Your mind pulls your left leg and your intuition pulls your "right". Gray clouds and clear skies wrapped into one. Vibrant colors sparkle and flicker, and your eyes say thank you. The search is over. Birth and death all at the same time. By choosing one you choose both.

Archives/2003

The 'hood

Shiny rims gleaming, trunks and license plates rattling under thunderous tunes. Shorts and halter tops sprinkle the sidewalks with delight. Some eye candy is sweet to the sight but bitter to the touch. Loose squares fill the air with a foul second hand odor and the butts become one with the landscape. Grandmas prepare food for the soul while grandsons cook up food for the pipes. Presidential elections held daily as Benjamin Franklin seems to hold the popular vote. War stories escape through the mouths of the young and young minded. Some filled with victory, yet more often defeat followed with statements of revenge captivate the listening ears. Sirens accompanied by flashing lights are a normal routine. There need not be an absence of light for fireworks. The display of sparks and loud popping sounds don't entertain. Through all the despair and false hope, an up and coming doctor, architect, musician and humanitarian keeps a strangle hold on a dream. The innocent and the guilty are both victims.

Final Thoughts

Dear You,

I sincerely appreciate and thank you for taking the time to read my book! I truly hope you enjoyed reading this material. Please feel free and welcome to join my email list for updates on future volumes of the Book of Poems series and other titles in the making by leaving your name along with any authentic feedback positive/negative that you have. I'd love to hear from you.
reviews@love4poems.com

All the very best,

Edem

Acknowledgments

I'd like to give a tremendous THANK YOU to the Universe. I would be nowhere near this point in my life without your guidance and blessings. I continue to learn daily that being present in every moment is paramount to my success in life.

Huge THANK YOU to all the people in my life past and present that have given me jewels of wisdom. Although many of you have passed on, your words and teachings will live on through me.

About the Author

Author's Name: Edem Y. Agbley

On March 6, 1980 in the city of Chicago, Edem Agbley was born. Edem Agbley was the only child born from two parents of Ghanaian descent making him a 1st generation American. Hip Hop culture was embraced by Edem at an early age through music, break dancing, and graffiti and was influential in his writings which he started to engage in beginning in 1996. In the 90's, Edem also had the opportunity to experience living in the Pacific Northwest with his mother in between living with his father back in the Midwest. Fortunately, Edem has the experience of many different cultures as he traveled the world in his early years with his mother. Edem, also being a supporter of theater, briefly in his early 20's pursued an acting career doing a few stage plays and independent films. Nowadays, Edem participates in transformational work which also involves the youth, and is an investor in various fields of business.

About LIVE SMART SOLUTIONS LLC

LIVE SMART SOLUTIONS LLC
You can learn more about the company at the following online location:
http://livesmartsolutionsllc.com/

www.ingramcontent.com/pod-product-compliance
Lightning Source LLC
Chambersburg PA
CBHW031659040426
42453CB00006B/351